DIY Woodworking Projects

17 Easy Woodworking Projects For Beginners

Table of contents

Introduction

You see them at craft fairs, or in the home decorating stores. Even in the usual places like Walmart and Target have them... Handmade wooden items that look beautiful in the store, but would look even better in your home.

Then you see the price. Ouch. Well-deserved when you realize the talent that goes into each piece, but who can afford that? And again, furniture and other things you have around your home have so much more meaning when they are made with your own hands.

If you are able to make your own furniture, or some other piece that you can out around your home, you will be able to enjoy it yourself for years to come, but you will also have a piece you can give to your children, and their children.

Before you know it you will have pieces that will be in the family for generations, or you will have the perfect thing to put in whatever room you want it in. One of the biggest benefits that comes from making things with your own hands is the fact that everything is entirely custom.

No matter what you want to make, you will be able to make it with ease, and you can make it to suit whatever you have in mind. There will be nothing holding you back when it comes to that new side table, or that bedframe.

What about a toy box for the kids? Easy, and it can be as big as you want it to be, and match anything you want it to. There is no end to the possibilities of what you can make.

But I don't know how to work with wood... you tell yourself. Don't worry. This book is your easy guide to making all kinds of easy projects... perfect for the beginner.

In no time at all you will be making whatever you like. When you see wood, you will no longer see a board, you will see a project waiting to be made, and a new piece that is just destined to be in your home.

What are you waiting for? Pick up that hammer, and head out to the old shed. There is a world of wood waiting for you to leave your notch on the door.

Toy Box

What you will need:

- 5 pieces of plywood, each one 4 ft x 4 ft
- A handsaw or table saw
- Screws
- Electric screwdriver
- 16 4x4 boards

Directions:

Cut one foot off of 3 pieces of plywood. Then, cut 2 feet off each of the other two pieces.

Don't skip on getting 5 pieces, there are times when the wood splits, even when you are a beginner, and you don't want to be short. Once you have all of the pieces, screw them together in the form of a box.

Leave the top open, there will be no lid unless you want to make an extra piece. Lids can be difficult with hinges, and they may catch little fingers, but it is entirely up to you if you want one.

Whether you do or don't have a lid, you still want to put on a border. Use the 4x4 pieces that you have, and cut them down to the size you need for your borders, and screw them on to the borders of the box.

Sand down the outside of the wood to cut down drastically on splinters, and there you have it.

Your little one's toy box is ready to go, and for years to come will happily hold on to all kinds of little treasures for whatever little one wants to keep their things safe and sound.

Flower Box

What you will need:

- 4 small boards.
- 1 piece, of plywood, 1 foot wide by 2 feet long
- Nails
- 8 4x4 boards
- Handsaw
- Hammer
- Screwdriver

Directions:

Nail the four boards up on the corner of the plywood, much like an upside down table. Next, cut the other boards to the length of the plywood, and nail on to the boards to form a box.

Take the screwdriver, and screw holes into the bottom of the flower box, these will allow for drainage. That's it! Now it is ready to fill with soil, and your favorite flower seeds.

Make sure you put in enough holes on the bottom piece of wood for it to be effective in draining. Too much water will kill the plants, and sitting on the wood could potentially cause it to become moldy or rot.

You can even add holes into the side boards, just to make sure they are helping in the draining process. When you pack in the flowers, make sure they are nice and firm in the top, this way you won't have to worry about extra dirt falling out of the sides.

Little things like that may seem like they are irrelevant to the rest of the project, but they will really add up in the long run. A little extra time right now is more than worth it later on.

Decorative Sign

What you will need:

- Fancy, thin piece of wood, not plywood
- Small hinge
- Wood burning tool
- Nails
- Hammer

Directions:

Heat the wood burning tool, and burn onto the wood whatever design or phrase you would like. If you are not a good artist free hand, you can always trace a design onto the wood, then burn over the lines.

Once it is well burned, turn the board over, and take the hinge and small nails. Nail the hinge onto the wood, then take a smaller piece of wood, and nail that to the other side of the hinge.

When it is complete, you can slide the hinge back and forth and make the decoration stand up by itself.

That's it. Place it in a prime location for you to enjoy whenever you are in the room. You can put anything on it, whether it be an inspirational quote, something funny, or even a design that you came up with.

Even if you just let your hand flow free with the burner, you will come up with stunning results that look incredible on any kind of wood finish. Adding a layer of wood finish to the finished project will also help it stay fresh and beautiful for years to come.

Picture Frame

What you will need:

- Nails
- 4 pieces of wood, cut to the size of the frame
- Wood glue
- Hammer
- Piece of glass to fit in the frame

Directions:

Lay out the pieces of wood to nail into a square (or rectangle) for the frame. This is easier if you nail two pieces, then the other two, then nail them together.

Take the piece of glass and set it in the frame. Use the wood glue to glue it in place, taking care not to get any in the main part of the glass.

Let the glass dry, and your picture frame is ready to hold onto memories for years to come. Make it as authentic as your trip. Using different kinds of wood makes for drastically different kinds of picture frames.

Barn wood is great if you want a truly rustic look, but there are all kinds of more polished woods you can use to make the best memories shine out even more.

Insider's tip: Try using a different stain on different kinds of wood. This will bring out their best qualities when you don't know what you are going for in particular. What makes it even better is you can seal in colors and make beautiful pieces that will perfectly compliment the day you had.

Shelves

What you will need:

- Thin pieces of wood, cut to the size you want your shelf to be
- Shelf hangers
- Nails
- Hammers
- Stud finder
- Sandpaper
- Finish

Directions:

Sand your boards, however many of them you have, and make the edges rounded and smooth. Next, treat them with the wood finish that you have.

Let them dry, according to the instructions. As the shelves are drying, use a stud finder to find the most secure place on your walls. Nail the shelf hangers into place, or use screws if you are going to be putting heavy things on the shelves.

Next, nail, or screw, the shelves onto the shelf hangers. Once they are secure in place, and completely dry, you are ready to go!

Shelves may seem to be ridiculously easy to make, but there is no end to the different variations you can do, and you can store all kinds of different things on them. These shelves here are not just indoor shelves, use them out in the shop, the garage, or anywhere you need to get things up off the floor and onto the walls.

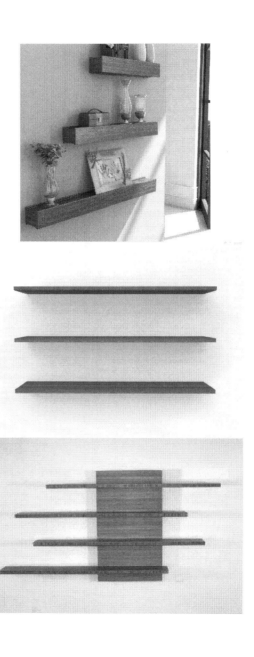

Easy Step Ladder

What you will need:

- Two boards, each 4 inches wide by 7 feet long
- Handsaw
- Screws
- 18 small boards, 4 inches wide by 2 feet long

Directions:

Use the saw and saw off the bottoms of both long lengths of wood, at the same angle so they lay flat on the floor when leaned against something.

Now, take each of the pieces of wood, and screw them along the side of one of the lengths of wood. These are going to be the steps, so make sure you have as many as you need.

This may mean that you need more than what we called for, but that's ok. Once they are all secure, lay the other length of wood over them, and screw the other sides.

Make sure it is all secure before use, and you are ready to go!

Insider's tip: There are plenty of different kinds of rubber ends you can get to attach to the base of your ladder. These will make it better for the bottom to stay in place when you are using it, and make it a lot safer for you.

You can also adjust the length of the ladder based on the length of board you use for the base. Don't be afraid to make it longer or shorter depending on what you need, just make sure you put on enough steps to make it safe to go up and down.

Picnic Table

What you will need:

- 12 boards, 6 feet long by 5 inches wide
- Screws
- Screwdriver
- Handsaw
- 4 boards, 4 inches wide by 4 feet long
- 2 boards, 2 feet long by 4 inches wide
- Stain

Directions:

Stain all of the wood. Make sure it is completely dry before you begin. Once you are ready, lay out the boards so you have an idea of what you want the finished project to look like, and build from there.

For starters, take 8 of the 6 foot boards, and lay them flat across 1 of your 2 by 4 boards. Securely screw them in place. Then do the same with the other side.

Next, take your handsaw, and saw at an angle on the 4 boards that are 4 feet long. Saw the angles so the top of the table can lay flat on the boards, and so the boards lay flat on the ground.

Once you have finished with this, take your handsaw again, and make a notch on all 4 boards, in the same place up on the board. This is where the bench is going to sit when it is all together.

Now, screw each of the legs to the table top, and flip over, so the legs are on the ground. It should really look like a table at this point. Now, attach the remaining long boards to the legs, making benches.

Add a final layer of stain to the wood when you are finished, and, if you would like to add more support to the frame, attach an additional board to each side of the table, and pulling the legs of the bench together.

That's it! Now all you have to do is sit down, and make some good memories with some good people!

Insider's tip: If you would like to make the table's edges more rounded, take a piece of sandpaper and sand off the edges before you put the table together. This is a good idea especially if you have small children that are likely to run their hands over the table.

Don't use plywood for this project. Plywood is too flimsy, and it leaves a lot of splinters. If you need to, custom order some boards that are the length you need. This will cost a little more up front, but it will save a lot of headache in the long run.

You can also modify this table to be a kids table if you shorten the lengths of the boards you are using. Just make sure you keep the dimensions the same, and you can make the table as short or as long as you want it.

Book Shelf

What you will need:

- 4 boards, 1 foot by 3 feet
- 2 boards, 6 inches by 5 feet
- Handsaw
- Paint
- Paintbrush
- Screwdriver
- Screws

Directions:

You have a lot of options when it comes to a bookshelf. The very first, and probably the easiest is to use one that is already made, and refurbish it. There is nothing wrong with taking something that has been made, and making it into something better, but we are going to look at starting completely from scratch on this one.

If you want to make your bookshelf funky, take the handsaw, and saw in some waves into the boards that are 6 inches by 5 feet. When you are done, you can attach the shelves.

This is simple, all you have to do is screw them in, keeping them level all the way across. You can do this on any design you saw into the wood, or you can keep it a lot more traditional and keep the legs straight.

Once everything is screwed together, you can paint the wood however you want it to look. Some people choose to make it artistic and paint it all kinds of colors, others decide to let the natural look of the wood stand out, and only stain it when they are finished.

Whatever you decide to do, painting is the final step before you can use it! Before you paint, sand down the rough edges to make sure the paint is applied evenly, and put on a nice layer all over the shelf before you continue.

Let the paint dry completely, and you are ready to put your new shelf to use! Whether it be for holding knick knacks, books, or whatever you want, this bookshelf is sure to stand up to the challenge!

Wooden Door

What you will need:

- 1 solid board, measuring the height and width of your doorway
- Stain
- Hinges
- Screwdriver
- Wood burning tool
- Screws
- Brush
- Sandpaper

Directions:

This is one solid piece of wood, but it isn't hard to come by. Simply measure the doorway you want to put a door in, and go to your hardware store and make the specifications.

They will use whatever wood you want, and they will make it the size that you need. We recommend you use oak, the finish is nice, and it responds well to the wood burning.

Once you have decided on the wood that you want, and you have your piece, you are ready to begin. Sand all of the wood smooth. Make sure there are no splinters standing up, or cracks that can be seen.

Now, take your burner, and follow carefully the design of panels on the door. If you are not good with free hand, you can always trace the pattern onto the door first, then copy that with your burner.

Once you have all of the design burned in, start again at the beginning and go over it again. This is going to be designed to last a lifetime, so you don't want to have to worry about it fading out of the door.

When it is complete, take the stain and the brush, and stain the whole door. You can put the design on both sides, depending on what room of the house it is, or you can stick with one side. When you are finished, however, you need to stain the whole door.

Now, attach to the hinges, and place in the doorway of your choosing. Attach a regular nob, or use one of the fancier ones, depending on what look you want to go for.

If you are making a door to a specialized room, such as the laundry room, pantry, or any of those, you can always burn the title in to the top of the door as well. You can even consider burning in designs to represent whichever room you are talking about.

Burn in a loaf of bread for the pantry, or some linen for the laundry room. Use your imagination, and make this a beautiful door that will adorn your home for years and years to come.

Bed Frames

What you will need:

- 4 post boards
- 2 5 foot boards,
- 2 8 foot boards
- 5 4 foot boards
- Screws
- Stain
- Brush
- Screwdriver
- Saw

Directions:

Cut the tops off of the post boards, making them the height you want them to be. You can do this making a headboard, but this pattern is for standard bedframes.

Once you have the post boards to the desired height, sand them down so they are smooth. Now, take the 5 foot boards, and screw them to the post boards. Now you should have to H shapes, with the cross of the H being low on the frame.

Next, take the 8 foot boards, and place them on the outside of the H shapes you have. Screw them in place to make a large Rectangle. Now take the 4 foot boards, and place them on the inside of this triangle, screwing them top and bottom to either side of the long boards.

Once you have all of the boards screwed together, sand off all of the edges. You don't want to have any rough edges here. This is important for those bare feet that are going to be in bed!

Once you are certain all is tight and secure, you can add in that final brushing of stain. This needs to dry completely, then you are ready to put on your mattress, and make your bed nice and neat!

Coffee Table

What you will need:

- 1 board, 3 feet by 2 feet
- Screws
- Screwdriver
- Paint
- Saw
- 4 boards, 4 inches by 18 inches
- Stain

Directions:

Begin by sanding all of the rough spots on the wood. You want this to be as smooth as you can get it. Once you are certain all of your pieces are well sanded, stain them.

Set them out to dry, and don't move on in the project until they are. Once they are ready to go, take your saw and saw off the tops of the short boards. Make sure they are all of equal length, and place the boards equally apart on the bottom of the flat board.

Take your screwdriver, and screw the legs on, making them firm against the bottom of the board. Again, sand off the rough edges that may have formed when you were working here, and turn the right side up.

Now you are ready for the fun part, painting. Take your brush, and paint your table in whatever color best matches your room. It can be solid and go with the walls, or you can go bold with it.

The best part of making anything homemade is that you can make it entirely custom, and that means there are no rules you need to follow when it comes to how something is going to look.

When you are finished painting, let it dry for a day, then add a second coat of paint. Coffee tables get a lot of action, you don't want your paint to start peeling because there wasn't enough of it on there!

Step Stools

What you will need:

- 2 boars, 1 foot by 1 foot
- 8 boards, 4 inches by 2 feet
- 8 boards, 4 inches by 1 foot
- Stain
- Screws
- Sandpaper
- Screwdriver

Directions:

Sand each of your pieces thoroughly, paying special attention to the flat piece. This is the part you are going to stand on, you want it to be as smooth as possible.

Next, take your screwdriver and screw the 2 foot boards to the bottoms of the flat boards. One on each corner, 4 per flat board. Then, take the remaining short boards, and screw them to the legs of the stools, halfway up the leg.

It is very important that these are all secure, this is what you are going to be trusting to hold you up when you are trying to reach something. When you are absolutely certain everything is secure, and screwed in place, it is time for the final stain.

Take your brush, and stain the entire stool, even on the underside where no one sees it. Once they are dry, you are ready to use them.

Pretty and functional, these stools are perfect no matter what you want to use them for, and you don't have to put them away when they are not in use, they are pretty enough for company!

Plates and Dishes

What you will need:

- Flat boards, various sizes
- Stain
- Brush
- Sandpaper
- Electric sander
- Saw

Directions:

Dishes and plates are a beautiful way to express your wooden talents. They are a little different than other things you make, in that they are entirely custom. To make a standard dish, do the following:

Take your saw, and cut the wood down to the size you want your dish to be. Next, cut it a little more intricately and make it the shape you want it to be as well.

Now, take your sander, and sand the wood into the dish you want it to be. A shallow groove for a plate, a deeper groove for a bowl. After you have your groove sanded in, take the hand sandpaper, and sand it down the rest of the way.

This is going to take a lot of time and patience, but it is worth it in the end. When you are happy with the shape, stain each piece and set them out to dry.

Note: Wooden plates and bowls don't like to be soaked. When you use them, wash them immediately to avoid swelling and other problems with your dish.

Garden Bench

What you will need:

- 4 boards, 2 feet by 5 feet
- 2 boards, 2 inches by 2 feet
- 4 boards, 4 inches by 3 feet
- 2 boards, 6 inches by 5 feet
- 2 boards, 3 inches by 18 inches
- Screws
- Screwdriver
- Paint

Directions:

Start by cutting 2 of your 5 foot boards down to the width of 18 inches. Now, take those 2 boards, and screw them onto the 2 boards that are 3 inches by 18 inches.

Now, take your other board, and screw that one to the board that is screwed to the 3 inch boards at a right angle. From there, attach the 2 inch by 2 feet boards. When those are in place, screw on the remaining 2 feet by 5 feet boards.

You should now have a seat shape that is really long, but no legs. When you are ready, take the 4 inch boards and screw them at an angle to the bottom of the bench. Take a saw and make it so they lie flat.

Make sure all of the screws are in place, and paint the bench the color that best matches your garden.

Square Shelves

What you will need:

- 4 boards, 4 inches wide by 6 inches long
- 4 boards, 4 inches wide by 5 inches long
- Wood glue
- Paint

Directions:

These are really easy to make. All you need to do is paint the boards the color of your choice. This can be the same color for all of them, or different colors per board, just make sure the colors look good together.

Once it is all dry, take the wood glue, and glue the boards together, forming a box shape. Make sure you line them up properly, so the right board is above the right thing, and the sizes aren't off.

When the glue is dry, you are ready to hang them!

Square shelves are a fun and unique way to express yourself. You can put them low enough on the wall that the inner shelf can be used as well as the one that is on top!

Entertainment Center

What you will need:

- An old entertainment center
- Hammer
- Nails
- Boards of various sizes
- Wood glue
- Paint

Directions:

Take all of the shelves off of the entertainment center. Now, take your boards, and cut them so you can make box shelves. Add these in place of the shelves that were there to begin with.

Next, remove the doors for the cupboards, and place shelves in there. Add in holes for cords where necessary, and make special places for all of your gaming systems.

Take the paint, and cover the entire entertainment center, so you can't tell what is old and what is new. Let dry, and add a second coat to the shelves. Once that is dry, you are ready to go!

Cute Path Markers

What you will need:

- Garden stakes
- Nails
- Hammer
- Wood burning tool
- Stain
- Small, flat boards

Directions:

Very simple and easy to do, these are supposed to look old fashioned. If you want to make an even more rustic look, use larger nails, but only if there is no danger of someone catching themselves on it.

Nail the top of the flat boards to the stakes, and lay on a table. Next, take your wood burner, and burn in cute sayings and directions into the flat board. Make sure the burns are in deep.

Burning tends to fade out of the wood if you are not deep enough, and that won't work for your signs! Once you have the burning in, set out the signs along your garden path, or even the walkway to your house!

Steps

What you will need:

- 3 flat boards, 1 foot by 2 feet
- 2 flat boards, 3 feet by 3 feet
- 1 flat board, 2 feet by 3 feet
- Sandpaper
- Stain

Directions:

Cut stair shapes out of the flat boards that are square. Make each step 1 foot higher than the rest.

Next, screw the tops of the boards that are 1 foot by 2 feet onto the top part of each step on your cutout.

When that is finished, screw the back piece on. Sand everything down nice and smooth, then stain.

These steps may be a little loud to step on, but you can mute the noise by adding carpet to the top of the steps you put on. Or, you can screw more wood inside the steps to help absorb the noise.

Either way, these are an easy thing to pack along to help smaller travelers get in and out of vehicles, or to make it easier for pets to get up on the bed.

Treasure Box

What you will need:

- Small saw
- Stain
- 1 piece of wood, 1 foot by 1 foot
- Small nails
- Small hammer

Directions:

Take your saw, and cut out 2 pieces of wood that are 2 inches by 3 inches. Next, cut out 2 pieces that are 2 inches by 4 inches. Finally, cut out 2 pieces that are 4 inches by three inches.

Take your hammer, and nail the 4 smaller pieces onto one bigger piece, this is the box, only without the lid. Purchase 2 small hinges, and using the small hammer, nail the hinges onto the lid of the box, and onto the back of the box.

Sand down the whole thing until it is smooth, and stain it with a red stain. If you are feeling really creative, take your wood burning tool and burn in a name or a design.

The perfect place to keep your small treasures, or the perfect gift for your friend, this charming little box will keep everything locked away!

Dish Drainer

What you will need:

- 6 6 inch dowels
- 2 pieces of wood, 2 inches by 8 inches
- 4 rubber stoppers
- 2 handles
- Drill
- Wood glue

Directions:

Drill holes into the 2 pieces of wood, spaced evenly apart. Dip the ends of the dowels in the wood glue, and place in the holes. Let dry. Next, attach the handles to the top of the pieces of wood, and the stoppers to the bottom, spaced out one in each corner.

Place on a towel or in your sink, and you are ready to dry those dishes! A classy, yet refined way of drying the dishes, this drainer will make it look like you are in the cabins, even in the comfort of your own home!

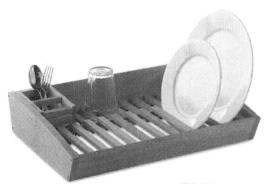

Conclusion

There you have it. Twenty easy to make woodworking projects. No matter what the occasion is, or what you need in your home, you now have the skills to make it yourself, and to make it your own.

There is no end to the possibilities of what you can make. All you need is wood, a hammer, and some nails, and you can make whatever your heart desires. That picture frame to cover that perfect moment? Got it.

That new set of bed frames for the grandkids? No problem. When you have the ability to make things with your hands, everything becomes a project just waiting for you to make your mark on it.

Even when you are out in the woods, or when you are looking through the old pieces at the thrift store, you will be able to see how you can make these old things your own.

What makes this all even better is the fact you now have been able to use power tools, and other woodworking tools to make your projects. This means that even home repairs are going to be that much easier for you, now that you know what you are doing around the shed!

I hope you were able to learn everything you needed in this book, and I know that you are now able to go out there and make whatever it is you want to make. There's no such thing as impossible. Use your imagination and your skills, and you can have whatever you want to make.

Made in the USA
Middletown, DE
16 November 2022

15239765R00027